WORK

by Sally M. Walker and Roseann Feldmann
photographs by Andy King

Lerner Publications Company • Minneapolis

BE A WORD DETECTIVE

Can you find these words as you read about work?
Be a detective and try to figure out what they mean.
You can turn to the glossary on page 46 for help.

axle

complicated machine

force

friction

inclined plane

lever

machine

pulley

screw

simple machine

wedge

work

Chapter 1

We're getting ready for an adventure! Alex and Danielle put snacks in a bag.

WORK

It's Saturday! There is no school today.
We're going on an adventure. We are going to
look for animals at the park.

First, we pack some yummy snacks. Then we get a rope and some other things that we need. We put everything into a box. We're set and ready to go. It's time to lift the box.

 ZZ and Hipocito load stuff into a box.

Whoops! We may have packed too much. The box is too heavy. We can't carry it far.

We do work every time we move an object to a new place. We don't mind doing some work. But it would be a lot of work to carry the box to the door. We need to make the work easier. What shall we do?

The box is very heavy. We can't carry it all the way to the park.

We can slide the box across the floor.

Lifting the box is too hard. We can use force to slide the box instead. Force is a push or a pull. We take turns pushing and pulling the box across the carpet. Our pushes and pulls are strong forces. But the box moves slowly. It moves only a few inches at a time.

The box moves slowly because of friction. Friction is a force between the box and the bumpy carpet. Friction resists our pushes and pulls. It stops or slows moving objects. There is a lot of friction between the box and the carpet. But soon we won't have to push and pull as hard. We know there will be less friction on the wood floor.

It's hard to slide the box on the carpet.

It's easy to slide the box on the smooth wood floor.

We push the box onto the wood floor. Here the floor is smooth. It is almost like ice. There is less friction between the box and the shiny wood floor. The box slides quickly toward the door.

Chapter 2

SIMPLE MACHINES

Dragging the box down the front walk is hard work. The concrete is very rough and bumpy. There's a lot of friction between the bottom of the box and the front walk. Moving the box a short distance makes us tired.

We can't carry the box all the way to the park. It would be too much work. We need to use a machine. A machine is a tool that makes work easier.

The front walk is very rough. It's hard to push the box.

We can't slide our box all the way to the park. That would be too much work!

If we used a car, we could get the box to the park quickly. Our work would be really easy! But a car is a complicated machine. A car has

lots of moving parts. It would be hard to use.
And we are not old enough to drive. We need a
simple machine. What shall we use?

 *ZZ has an idea. She knows an easy way to take
our stuff to the park.*

I know! We can use a wagon! Our wagon is made with a simple machine called a wheel and axle. An axle is a bar that goes through the center of a wheel. When the wheels turn, our wagon moves along the sidewalk. Each wheel touches the sidewalk in only one small spot. So there is almost no friction.

We load our box into the wagon.

Pulling the wagon is easy!

The wagon is a perfect way to get our box to the park. The wagon's wheels and axles will make our work easier. That way, we won't be tired when we get to the park. We load the box into the wagon. The wagon's wheels and axles make it easier and faster to get our work done.

ZZ and Hipocito helped us bring our stuff to the park. But now they have gone to play baseball. We will find them later.

Chapter 3

IN THE PARK

ZZ and Hipocito have gone to play baseball. But Ryan and Michael will be joining us for our adventure.

Here comes Ryan! He is wearing in-line skates. The wheels on his skates spin quickly. Skating fast is fun. But now Ryan needs to stop. He rolls onto the grass. Friction between his skates and the bumpy grass slows him down. Stopping is easy. Ryan sits down and takes off his skates.

Skating onto the grass helps Ryan slow down.

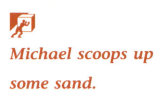

Michael scoops up some sand.

Alex sees something new. It's a pulley! A pulley is a wheel that has a rope looped around it. The rope fits in a groove around the edge of the wheel. A pulley is a great way to lift a scoop of sand. We can't wait to try it.

Michael stays on the ground. Alex and Ryan climb to the top. Michael fills the scoop with

sand. The scoop is tied to a rope. The rope is looped around the pulley. When Alex pulls down on the rope, the scoop goes up. Ryan grabs the scoop. He passes it to Alex. She pours the sand into a funnel. The sand goes through the funnel and back down to the ground. Using the pulley is much easier than carrying the scoop up and down. It's more fun, too.

Alex pulls down on the rope. Now Ryan can grab the scoop full of sand.

A slide is a simple machine called an inclined plane.

The top of the fort is a good home base. It is a great place to put our stuff. But we can't climb up holding the heavy box. And we don't want to make a lot of trips. That's too much work. We need another simple machine. What shall we use?

I know! We can use the slide! A slide is a simple machine called an inclined plane. An inclined plane is a sloping surface. The slide's

surface is smooth and slanted. There is hardly any friction. It's perfect for lifting our box.

We tie the rope around the box. We pull the rope hand over hand. We pull the box up the slide. Now all our stuff is up in the fort. And we're not tired at all. The inclined plane made our work much easier. We have plenty of energy left for our adventure.

 Ryan pulls the rope, and the box goes up the slide.

Ryan gives Alex a ride in the wagon.

Chapter 4
SAFARI

It's time to look for animals. We load a few things in the wagon. Then we're ready for our safari.

Alex rides in the wagon. She isn't doing work. But Ryan is working hard. He is using force to move Alex a great distance.

It's getting harder to pull the wagon. The ground must be slanting uphill a little. Ryan stops the wagon and Alex gets out.

It's too hard to pull Alex up the hill. She gets out of the wagon and walks.

When we let go of the wagon, it rolls back down the hill!

The empty wagon starts rolling. We grab the handle before it rolls far. But when we let go, the wagon rolls again. That is a problem. It isn't fun to run after the wagon. And no one wants to hold the handle. That would be boring. We need another simple machine. What shall we use?

I know! We can use pieces of bark! A piece of bark can be used as a simple machine. This

simple machine is called a wedge. Some chips of bark will solve our wagon problem.

We shove some bark behind each back wheel. The wheels roll up onto the bark a tiny bit. But then the bark pushes against the wheel. Its force makes the wheel stop. Our wagon doesn't roll away. It won't go anywhere until we remove those bark chip wedges. Now everyone can look for animals.

 Alex puts some bark behind the wagon's wheels.

*The pieces of bark are wedges. They keep our
wagon from rolling.*

Squirrels dash up a nearby tree. They chatter
loudly at us. A blue jay screeches as it flies
overhead. But these animals are not wild and
strange enough for us. Strange creatures live in
damp, dark places. We know it will be damp
and dark under the big rocks near our wagon.

We try to move one of the rocks. We push. We pull. But the rock does not move. It is very heavy. We would have to do a lot of work to move it. We need another simple machine. What shall we use?

The big rock is too heavy for us to lift.

Our baseball bat will help us to lift the heavy rock.

I know! We can use our baseball bat! A baseball bat can be used as a simple machine. This simple machine is called a lever. The lever will help us move the rock.

We shove the small end of the bat under the rock. Then we push downward. The bat goes all the way to the ground. The rock doesn't move at all. But we don't give up. We have an idea that may solve the problem.

Alex pushes down on the bat. But the rock still doesn't move.

We find a small rock. We put it under the bat, near the big rock. We push downward again. Now the bat lifts the big rock. Our bat and the small rock have made a good lever. We quickly put another small rock under the big rock. It keeps the big rock from falling.

Alex puts a small rock under the bat. She pushes down on the bat again. Now she can lift the big rock!

Many strange creatures live under the big rock.
Ryan uses a magnifying glass to see them better.

Lots of strange bugs are scurrying out from under the big rock. Our safari is a success!

It's time to go back to the fort.

Chapter 5

SNACK TIME

Our adventure has made us hungry. We decide to go back to the fort. We put the bat back in the wagon. We remove the wedges from the wagon's wheels.

Now we are going down the hill. We are rolling down an inclined plane. The hill is a simple machine. It makes pulling the wagon back to the fort faster and easier.

We climb the ladder to the fort. It's time for a snack.

We climb the ladder to the top of the fort.

If we had no teeth, it would be hard work to eat an apple. But we have simple machines in our mouths. The tips of our front teeth are wedges. When we bite, our teeth split the apple apart. They make the work of eating easier.

Working hard has made us very hungry!

Michael's front teeth are wedges. They help him bite into an apple.

Our container is filled with juice. The lid of the container is a simple machine. What kind of machine is it?

I know! The lid is a screw! The bumpy ridges on the lid are a simple machine called a screw. It would be a lot of work to pull the lid off. We would have to use our whole hand and our arm. It is much easier to unscrew the lid. We just turn the lid with our fingers.

The lid of our container is a screw. If we turn the lid until it's tight, the juice can't spill out.

Ryan carries the box down the slide.

It's getting late. We have to go home.
We screw the lid on, so the juice doesn't spill.
Then we put our trash and our other things
back in the box. We slide the box down the
inclined plane. Then we load the wagon. We
say good-bye to Ryan and Michael. We find ZZ
and Hipocito. And we head for home.

We leave the park and head for home.

Chapter 6
MAKING WORK EASIER

We did a lot of work today. Every time we moved an object to a new place, we did work. But we had plenty of energy to do all the work. Simple machines made the work easier. They helped us do the work faster, too.

It has been a fun day. It was fun because we used simple machines. The machines saved us time and energy.

 Hipocito pulls the wagon up the front walk.

We rest on the front steps before putting our
stuff away. We talk about our adventure.

People who use simple machines can do
their work more easily. And they can work
faster. Using machines gives us an advantage.
An advantage is a better chance of completing
our work. Using a simple machine is almost
like having a helper. We don't have to do all
the work. And that is a big advantage.

We like having an advantage. The next time we go on an adventure, we will use simple machines again. We will use them every time we have to do work. What will you use?

 Simple machines make work much easier!

ON SHARING A BOOK

When you share a book with a child, you show that reading is important. To get the most out of the experience, read in a comfortable, quiet place. Turn off the television and limit other distractions, such as telephone calls. Be prepared to start slowly. Take turns reading parts of this book. Stop occasionally and discuss what you're reading. Talk about the photographs. If the child begins to lose interest, stop reading. When you pick up the book again, revisit the parts you have already read.

Be a Vocabulary Detective

The word list on page 5 contains words that are important in understanding the topic of this book. Be word detectives and search for the words as you read the book together. Talk about what the words mean and how they are used in the sentence. Do any of these words have more than one meaning? You will find the words defined in a glossary on page 46.

What about Questions?

Use questions to make sure the child understands the information in this book. Here are some suggestions:

What did this paragraph tell us? What does this picture show? What do you think we'll learn about next? If you push against a tree, but the tree does not move, have you done work? Why/Why not? Which has more friction, a rough surface or a smooth surface? How many kinds of simple machines can you name? What is your favorite part of the book? Why?

If the child has questions, don't hesitate to respond with questions of your own, such as: What do *you* think? Why? What is it that you don't know? If the child can't remember certain facts, turn to the index.

Introducing the Index

The index helps readers find information without searching through the whole book. Turn to the index on page 47. Choose an entry such as *friction* and ask the child to use the index to find out how friction makes work harder. Repeat with as many entries as you like. Ask the child to point out the differences between an index and a glossary. (The index helps readers find information, while the glossary tells readers what words mean.)

SIMPLE MACHINES

Books

Baker, Wendy, and Andrew Haslam. *Machines*. **New York: Two-Can Publishing Ltd., 1993.** This book offers many fun educational activities that explore simple machines.

Burnie, David. *Machines: How They Work*. **New York: Dorling Kindersley, 1994.** Beginning with descriptions of simple machines, Burnie goes on to explore complicated machines and how they work.

Hodge, Deborah. *Simple Machines*. **Toronto: Kids Can Press Ltd., 1998.** This collection of experiments shows readers how to build their own simple machines using household items.

Van Cleave, Janice. *Janice Van Cleave's Machines: Mind-boggling Experiments You Can Turn into Science Fair Projects*. **New York: John Wiley & Sons, Inc.: 1993.** Van Cleave encourages readers to use experiments to explore how simple machines make doing work easier.

Ward, Alan. *Machines at Work*. **New York: Franklin Watts, 1993.** This book describes simple machines and introduces the concept of complicated machines. Many helpful experiments are included.

Websites

Brainpop—Simple Machines
<http://www.brainpop.com/tech/simplemachines/> This site has visually appealing pages about levers and inclined planes. Each page features a movie, cartoons, a quiz, history, and activities.

Simple Machines
<http://sln.fi.edu/qa97/spotlight3/spotlight3.html> With brief information about all six simple machines, this site provides helpful links related to each and features experiments for some of them.

Simple Machines—Basic Quiz
<http://www.quia.com/tq/101964.html> This challenging interactive quiz allows budding physicists to test their knowledge of work and simple machines.

45

GLOSSARY

axle: a bar that goes through the center of a wheel

complicated machine: a machine that has many moving parts

force: a push or a pull

friction: a force caused when two objects rub together. Friction stops or slows moving objects.

inclined plane: a sloping surface

lever: a stiff bar that is used to move other objects

machine: a tool that makes work easier

pulley: a wheel that has a rope looped around it. The rope fits in a groove around the edge of the wheel.

screw: a fastener that has bumpy ridges winding around it. The lid of a jar is a screw.

simple machine: a machine that has few moving parts

wedge: an object that is thin at one end and thick at the other. Your front teeth are wedges.

work: moving an object from one place to another

INDEX

Pages listed in **bold** type refer to photographs.

complicated machines, 14–15

force, 9, 27
friction, 10–11, 12, 16, 19, 23

inclined planes, 22–23, 35

levers, 30–32

machines, 13

pulleys, 20–21

screws, 38
simple machines, 16, 20–23, 26–27, 30, 38, 40–43

wedges, 26–27, **28,** 36, **37**
wheels and axles, 16–17, 19
work, 8, 17, 23, 24, 29, 36, 38, 40, 42–43

About the Authors

Sally M. Walker is the author of many books for young readers. When she isn't busy writing and doing research for books, Ms. Walker works as a children's literature consultant. She has taught children's literature at Northern Illinois University and has given presentations at many reading conferences. She lives in Illinois with her husband and two children.

Roseann Feldmann earned her B.A. degree in biology, chemistry, and education at the College of St. Francis and her M.S. in education from Northern Illinois University. As an educator, she has been a classroom teacher, college instructor, curriculum author, and administrator. She currently lives on six tree-filled acres in Illinois with her husband and two children.

About the Photographer

Freelance photographer Andy King lives in St. Paul, Minnesota, with his wife and daughter. Andy has done editorial photography, including several works for Lerner Publishing Group. Andy has also done commercial photography. In his free time, he plays basketball, rides his mountain bike, and takes pictures of his daughter.

METRIC CONVERSIONS

WHEN YOU KNOW:	MULTIPLY BY:	TO FIND:
miles	1.609	kilometers
feet	0.3048	meters
inches	2.54	centimeters
gallons	3.787	liters
tons	0.907	metric tons
pounds	0.454	kilograms

P9-CEB-300